Iowa Eccentrics

Michael Kramme

Published by Michael Kramme, 2023.

Dedicated to
Michael Zahs
For preserving the Brinton archives

CHAPTER ONE
JONATHAN BRINTON

God spoke to Jonathan Brinton. Several times.

In the earliest conversation, God revealed to Jonathan the meaning of the Lord's Prayer among other things. Jonathan felt the need to spread the word of his vision.

A notice appeared in the March 3, 1869, issue of the *Washington* (Iowa) *Press.*

Card from Mr. J. Brinton

2nd MONTH 28th, 1869

Editor Press: Wilt thou be so kind as to say in the paper that J. Brinton desires to speak to the people. Having been denied the privilege of the churches, he has hired Corette's Hall for the next, first day, it being the 7th day of the next month, where he will speak to those who are desirous to hear of a certain, vision, the interpretation thereof, an explanation of the Lord's Prayer, and other things as they may present themselves to his mind. All are invited but more particularly the Preachers. J. Brinton

A response to the meeting appeared in the March 10, 1869, issue of the paper.

Religious

Mr. J. Brinton's crazy religious harangues have made a monomaniac of his brother Edward. He stood on the street last evening and shouted many times "Bring out your guns!" and was not long in getting a crowd to hear his "message" which he ala John the Baptist, has as he claims, "from the Lord Almighty." The brothers inveigh against the practice of taking pay for preaching and against divers of sins of the churches. Do they mean to say that sermons have not market value.

The same column contained the following:

Mr. J. Brinton who has been retailing his black-cat alias Beelzebub vision in this town for the past two weeks, closed it out wholesale in Corette's Hall last Sunday p.m. He also interprets the Lord's Prayer, &c. He had placed only fifteen chairs on the platform for the accommodation of the preachers whom he specially invited to be present. Said chairs were vacant. He no doubt thinks our clergy are a timid set.

The March 17, issue contained the following:

Mr. J Brinton, who styles himself the "Lord's servant," is not in another card. He thinks the clergy and churches don't do right by him. If he can't "make the rifflle" this time, he will no doubt conclude that he ought to shake the dust off his feet against this place,

and be thrice convinced that there is a sacred rose born to blush unseen and waste his fragrance on the desert air.

A similar notice appeared in the March 19, 1869, issue of the *Washington Gazette*:

We received a lengthy communication from Jonathan Brinton, but in a few words, we can give the substance of what he desires. He is very anxious to speak to the people of this city on religious matters and is waiting with patience for an opportunity. It has been reported that he is insane; he strenuously asserts his sanity, and claims that he is only carrying out the will of his Master.

Jonathan Schofield Brinton, the son of John and Sarah Matlack Brinton, was born on June 2, 1818, in Allegheny County, Pennsylvania.

His great-great-great-great grandfather William Brinton was baptized on December 1, 1636 in Stratford, England. He and his wife immigrated to America and settled in Birmingham, Pennsylvania where he died in 1699 or 1700.

His great-great grandfather, George, filed a claim of 54 lbs. 11s, 8d for damages by the British at the Revolutionary War Battle of Brandywine.

Jonathan married Mary Dillon on January 29, 1846. They had seven children: Nathan Marshal

(1848-1919), Mary Louise (1850-1913), Sarah Ann (1852-1935), William Franklin (1857-1919), Rosanna C. (1859-?), George Henry (1862-1934), and Ella Alvina (1865-1945).

Jonathan received his education at Salem, Ohio, and taught school briefly before his marriage. The family settled in Brighton, Iowa, in 1843, returned to Pennsylvania in 1854 and back to Washington County in 1860.

The family may have moved back briefly to Allegheny County, Plum Township, Pennsylvania in 1868. However, they were back in Washington County, Iowa by 1869.

The following article appeared in the *Washington Press* on March 24, 1869:

STAND FROM UNDER!

Mr. Brinton, the religious enthusiast, feels it in his bones that a dire calamity hangs over this nation, and that something is going to drop. We submit to this ex-demonist that it can't be the "nigger," for we are fast the legislating the nitroglycerin combustible gun cotton-kerosene lamp explosive engendering chemists out of him. M. B suffers the millennium in the air, and says it's coming, but something's got to drop first. "Forewarned, forewarned."

Jonathan began a successful series of land speculations and purchases of military land grants. The Brintons owned land in the Grace Hill-Verdi-Brighton area southwest of the town of Washington. In 1851, they provided land and opera house seats for a new Christian Church in Brighton.

Jonathan was committed to the Iowa Hospital for the Insane, at Mt. Pleasant, Iowa. In a letter to Jonathan's wife Mary dated March 14, 1870, Mark Ranney, a member of the staff at the hospital wrote:

It's true your husband is uneasy and restless. And is by no means disposed to allow that there is any propriety in his being kept here at all. At the same time, I apprehend that his uneasiness comes more from his notion that there neither is nor ever has been any disturbance of his mind and is as much deposed to argue upon that question as he was disposed to argue and preach about religion, etc. etc. before he came here.

I suppose you of course believe you husband is and has been insane. I certainly do and I am firmly persuaded that the Hospital is the best place for a person who has been so unfortunate as to fall into such as state of mind.

I do not know as he is to get well, but I do believe in accordance with general experience, that his chances for getting better will be greater if his friend can have the patience and fortitude to follow out his present course of treatment long enough at the same time it is for them to determine how long he shall remain here or what course shall be pursued.

After his release on March 27, 1871, Jonathan sued Washington County for $435 "for illegal arrest and imprisonment by confinement in said Hospital at Mt. Pleasant for the term of 19 weeks. I was arrested by a mob of men consisting of Nathan Brinton, Henry Brinton (his sons) Marian Gallin and Benjamin McCoy."

The suit was dismissed due to a question of jurisdiction.

He did not agree with paying taxes, especially to support the railroads. On September 18, 1872, the *Washington Press* printed:

> Jonathan Brinton is posted for an argument on the Railroad bond tax, here, Sept 20, and challenges the county to meet him. We don't know his line of argument and are in doubt whether he has stolen the thunder of Mr. Robert Thompson.

He had a religious vision in 1874 in which he saw the hand of God directing his footsteps to Jerusalem that he might build an inn to prepare for the restoration of the Holy City. He first divided his property equally between himself and his wife, and then turned his face to the East. Upon arriving there, he purchased several acres near Jerusalem and erected a hotel. The adventure proved a successful and he later sent for his family. Many Englishmen and Americans stopped at the hotel, and it became one of the well-known places of Jerusalem. His family returned to America, and he went to London.

In a letter to his sons, he stated:

> I feel satisfied the Lord hath revealed to me great things to show to the people of the world and marvelous things to come yet to people unborn. As the prophets of old and the apostles of their days testified unto us at this day and period of the world and of things not yet done which is to be done and performed by the people that are yet to arrive from the birth and conception of the true seed of mankind to do all the will and pleasure of God.

Believed to be
a photograph
of Jonathan
in Jerusalem

Jonathan's wife and son Frank made frequent trips to Jerusalem trying to bring Jonathan back to Iowa. However, he said he would not return and pay taxes. Jonathan was always involved in business deals, he loaned money, sometimes at 12% interest.

Letters still survive from Jonathan, written in 1884 to his sons. Most of the content concerns money matters. He gives advice on running the farm and suggestions as to when to sell some of his property. In these letters, he frequently takes his wife and son to task for not providing him with money. He also repeatedly mentioned what he perceived as working against his welfare.

Now all you have to do is to obey my voice of instruction for I am able to give the best. Don't listen to mother, sister or brother. God requireth of children to obey their father first mother 2nd Elder brothers 3rd. If their Father is dead the mother comes then in command but as long as their father liveth his voice is to be first in command for the responsibility of their family's welfare rest on him as long as he liveth and I am now caring for your welfare and if I don't do what I know is right for you I must suffer for it and it stands me in hand to let you know that I am yet your father and claim you so long as you are willing to be cared for by me. But if you willfully rebels against my worth to you and deprive yourselves of all that I now possess or ever will possess it is all subject to my will and according as you are willing to hear me I will endeavor to give you the best council that you heed to better your welfare in life peace and happiness but if you will stand in and for your own ways you will have a hard life to live and a miserable death to die and you will have no one to blame for it but yourselves and the time is come for either union or disunion for I will hold no longerwith you in your folly trying to live there I shall claim what is in my name legal and offer it all for sale in a short time.

In another letter, to his family he continues:

London 4th 1884

I have not received any notice as to what I left in your care what is sold with who such and such articles was left.

I wrote to you a few days ago stating as I intend to carry out as soon as I possibly can and as little expense for I plainly can see that to depend on you any longer will be only a failure to me for I see your failure has clearly developed itself until you are in want yourselves, not having money enough to send me any without borrowing. I feel very sorry for you but what is done can't be helped now and it stands me in hand to alter the cause of your proceedings so that you will have to depend on your own resources not mine for I have had but a very poor chance to get ahead much for the want of means and help being as you all have forsaken me and don't nor seemingly won't listen to me anymore but are willing to listen to those of the basest sort that are only duping you to make gain of you to feed themselves. Where is that God told you of that he would give you more when you gave up all you had to them that mission thee entrusted thy house and lot with that has brought thee into the poverty stricken state thee is in and thee is now left houseless and penniless to grapple along back there to get a little more off of my land to feed their deluded subjects not only at thy expense but mine. And if I let you do so as you please, I will soon find myself in the same poor staring fire? I want you to give up your folly thinking that God

requireth not for you to feed the lazy idle boasters that say we trust all to God and are willing to rob you and me and everybody than can dup or overcome to believe in their foul stinking mesmeric Witchcraft in order to glut themselves of the fruit of my garden and use the water of the cistern that cost me so much money to get and labor but they can use all and say we trust all to God. Does God allow one people to take of the other for nothing but say as they do.

Letter from Jonathan Brinton to his sons

Jonathan was also an inventor and had secured a patent for a broom-making machine. He also had plans for a perpetual motion machine that he tried to get money for a patent and experimental model at the time of his disappearance.

Jonathan printed a broadsheet for distribution explaining his invention and inviting potential investors to contact him.

NOTICE IS HEREBY GIVEN

THATJOHNATHAN BRINTON,

ofJerusalem ,

Has gained a knowledge of

information on propelling power sufficient to propel all kinds of rotary machinery; and for the benefit of all wanting motive power to move machinery, either on water or land, it can be used, not costing anything after started but the necessary cost of keeping up repair of machinery. As it is perpetual, it can never be worn out, nor burnt up. Nor rot or rust away, nor consumed by use, nor destroyed in any conceivable manner; therefore is perpetual. It can be applied to all vessels floating on water, either small or large, and on land the same, turning everything needed that goes on wheels. And maybe used for ploughing and sowing, reaping and mowing, and all kinds of farming purposes, where there is no obstructions in the way, such as stones stumps, or trees, and the ground too uneven. The power cannot be patented, neither does it need man's protection. Man is not the inventor of it – it belongs to God; and it is now revealed to Jonathan Brinton to set this information before the people of the world to see if any there be that wants such a power to be used for the benefit of all living, to cheapen the necessaries of life; to aid the poor class, making all things more plentiful by the cheapness of transportation, on sea and land; in travel and moving materials with less cost, and to greater advantage, than the present mode. The right to use this power can only be by leave of Jonathan Brinton, or his appointed Agents; and all attempting to use this power without licence (sic), will be a trespasser against the God of all power, both on sea and land. And, Jonathan Brinton has the knowledge of a different hull or bottom of ships, or water craft, which is much superior to those now in use. They cause greater buoyancy on the water, and pass more easily over it, with greater safety and swiftness of speed than anything afloat. All is gained by a revelation of inspiration as revealed.

This Power will be leased by the year, paid in advance. On the receipt of the money the Licence (sic) will be sent to any address. It will be reckoned by the inch, for all sizes, and it will be certain to answer every purpose, as stated, when the necessary arrangements are made to carry it successfully on in the locality needed. Jonathan Brinton understands the theory of all its parts, but not having any chance as yet to get the necessary machinery made, will give any sailing ship building company the privilege to set it up on a small scale at a cost not exceeding $10.00, and deduct $10,000 out of the lease for using and the same for land machinery. The ship will do with single gearing of double; but the land ought to be double of a heavy power. All power wanted, can be put on for any purpose necessary, and can easily be managed. Harmless in its parts; safe at all times; no danger as to fire or explosion. The first applications attended to in rotation; as presented within three

months from the 1st of January; ad as soon as in successful operation to see all is right, the Licence (sic) will be issued, and the price of the lease require of all that want to use the said power, after being convinced as to its saving an usefulness.

All Newspapers copying this notice, and sending me a paper, will be entitled to a nice reward after it get successfully into operation, both in England and America. This Power can be easily attached to all sailing vessels now in use, giving power to steer as straight as steam ships, costing nothing but the necessary expense of the Power, to propel which is not half the expense of steam carrying freight in place of coal and heavy machinery.

All who take an interest in, and

require information on, this great Inspired discovery, are requested to send their address to JONATHAN BRINTON, No 11, Tomlin's Terrace, Salmon's Lane, Limehouse, E., enclosing three postage stamps, for expense of a reply.

Respectfully submitted to the people for an early reply.

JONATHAN BRINTON,
LONDON, ENGLAND.

Jonathan continued to write letters home demanding money and accusing his family of continued misdeeds. Many of the letters contained such rambling rants that the family had concerns for his sanity.

Suddenly the letters stopped arriving. Mary and Frank, concerned about Jonathan sailed to London to try to find him.

Frank posted "wanted posters" around Europe in hopes of finding his father. They discovered nothing about his last days and perhaps his death.

Mary Brinton died on April 26, 1902, at the home of her daughter Ella near Chapin, Iowa. The funeral was held in the home of her daughter

Sarah Ann in Washington, Iowa. She is buried in the family plot in Elm Grove Cemetery. Her obituary stated:

> Her Husband, Jonathan Brinton became impressed with the idea that Jerusalem was to be restored as a dwelling place for believers while the rest of the world would be destroyed. He was a great bible reader, and this was the interpretation he put upon the prophesies. After trying in vain to get his neighbors to accompany him to the hold land he, about 25 years ago, made the trip aloe. He took considerable money with him and bought property there, but the Arabs did not take kindly to him and he was compelled to leave that country. His wife and son Frank had followed him to that country, but after a night attack by the Arab robbers during which they had a narrow escape from death, they all decided to return to Iowa. On their way home Jonathan Brinton was lost and never after heard from.

Jonathan's cenotaph at Elm Grove Cemetery, Washington, Iowa, says, "Lost in London, England".

Mary Brinton's funeral procession

CHAPTER TWO
WILLIAM FRANKLIN BRINTON

William Franklin Brinton was born on July 12, 1856, in Westmorland, Pennsylvania. In 1860, his family moved to Washington County, Iowa. Frank grew up on a farm in the Grace Hill/Verdi area of Washington County.

He likely attended a one-room school named "Pleasant" near Grace Hill. It is doubtful that he attended beyond eighth grade. He grew up on the farm but was not interested in farming.

In 1880, Frank and his mother moved to Egypt to be with his father who had moved there in 1874. They lived there until 1883, when Frank and his mother returned to Iowa.

When his father moved to the Holy Land, Frank left the farming to his younger brother George. Frank and his mother made several later trips to the Holy Land to encourage Jonathan to return to Iowa. They heard from Jonathan in 1886 and traveled to London to try to locate him. They were unsuccessful, and they never heard from Jonathan again.

Frank made a study of the Middle East during his visits. He learned the language, music, and culture of the people of the Holy Land. While there, he took many magic lantern slides. Magic Lantern slides were projected on a screen for large audiences and became a form of popular entertainment.

When Frank returned to Iowa, he formed the Brinton Entertainment Company (See Chapter Four).

He began presenting magic lantern illustrated lectures about the Holy Land in area churches. He sang and wore Middle Eastern costumes His presentations proved popular and lucrative. He never returned to farming.

Frank Brinton in Costume

Frank
Brinton in a
Holy Land
costume used
in his
presentations

The Inventor

His father's interest in inventing greatly influenced him. Frank received patents for a Distance Power Excavating Machine, a Road Grader, a Means for Excavating and Transporting Material in Grading and a Distant Power Excavating Machine. In 1920, Frank received a patent for a rewinding means for motion pictures. This patent lists Frank as deceased, but included his wife, Indiana, and brother George as co-inventers.

Patent
drawing
for Brinton
invention

Frank also became interested in maned flight as early as 1890, and he made several model airships. (See Chapter 5)

Frank also invented a bicycle, but evidently did not patent the device.

Mr. Brinton also has another invention improved. It is a frame, which fits the back of a bicycle rider and saves the trouble of handlebars. The rider can lean back straight in this frame, and by swaying, the body guides the wheel. He has this seat arranged so that there is little difficulty in mounting. Heretofore the frame was in the way of the rider when mounting the wheel. Now he has it so arranged that the back will fold up to the rider's back after he has mounted.

Frank Brinton's bicycle

Still another theory is receiving the attention of the inventor. He believes that a round body will move on its own accord when extreme heat is applied on one side and

extreme cold on the other. To prove this, he places a stick about 12 feet long in a rim of a wheel. At one end of the stick he applies cold and at the other heat. This wheel, he says, will then turn once around in an hour.

Land Speculator

Frank first went to Texas in the spring of 1893... ".to ride out a cheap ticket which I got in Omaha, Nebr. I was like a great many other people who live in the north. I thought that Texas was the last place on earth for a person to live, but I hadn't been in the state very long until I changed my mind. Instead of finding it one of the worst places to live I found it one of the best, especially the Gulf Coast country."

In 1908, the Immigration Land Company of Des Moines, founded The Iowa Colony, located in Brazoria County, Texas. Frank purchased several acres of land there.

While on his first visit, he bought 600 acres at $8.00 per acre by 1913 he estimated that it was worth over $75 per acre.

He made additional trips to Texas and encouraged others to join the "Iowa Community"

> I hope to be able to raise a company of tourists that want to visit the south next September, and I want to bring them with me down into this part of the country and show them the great fields of rice being harvested, the orange, lemon and fig trees loaded with fruits, besides the hundreds of other interesting sights and the finest climate in the world.

On March 20, 1914, Frank placed a quarter-page advertisement in the *Washington Evening Journal* offering to sell or trade up to 640 acres in the Iowa Colony. In the advertisement he went into detail about the Colony including its officers and activities.

Frank married Indiana Putman on January 27, 1898 in Chicago with the Rev. A. C. Hirst presiding. She joined him in the Brinton Entertainment Company and traveled with him on the presentations.

Frank had strong religious views, which he often shared with the local newspapers. During a movement to establish a united universal Christian church, he wrote a lengthy essay in support of the project which appeared in *The Washington Evening Journal*, issue of March 28, 1912.

> I was much pleased when I read in your paper what was about to take place in Crookston, Minn., in regard to the union of the different churches being bought about by the Men and Religion Forward Movement. I have hoped that something good would come out of their work here in Washington and if they can only bring the different denominations here in Washington into one great body of Christian workers they will

have accomplished a great work. I have known for many years that the division of the Christian churches was not the highest standard of Christian work, nor is it according to Christ's teaching or the teaching of the bible. Let me say further that the creeds and sects have caused more strife and trouble than any one thing in the history of the world. I am not a Mohammedan, neither do I believe in their religion, but when it comes to brotherly love is their church they will put the Christians to shame.

After reading an article criticizing show people, he wrote a defense with several scripture allusions.

Mr. Brinton wants to know when a person or a number of persons have been Publicly slandered, and that put in Print, should the offended keep quiet and allow the public to think that the accused guilty, or should they make a defense stating the truth that the public might have a better chance to judge.

It has been announced that 50% of the traveling companies in theatrical work are immoral people and good Christian people shouldn't go to see or hear them. If this statement is true about the morality of these people, let us see from what (?) of the people got their start by reciting and singing songs at their mother's house. Later they were taken into the Church and

rehearsed that they might take part in Children's Day Program given in the church, later in Sunday School and Church entertainments, School Exhibitions, Commencements and home talent shows and in Colleges where the more talented were chosen to entertain, rehearse and put in companies and sent out to entertain in Churches.

As I 've seen here in Washington, haven't those been loudly applauded and encouraged in their work.

Frank and Indiana built a house at 921 South Iowa in Washington. The Washington Evening Journal reported in 1910 that the house would have a flat area on the roof for future airships to land. They also planned to install a solar system to heat the home and produce hot water. They planned to install glass lenses to focus sunlight on copper pipes. Another feature of the house was to have a garage in the basement. After Indiana's death, the house was remodeled into apartments and would be almost unrecognizable to the Brintons today.

The Brintons standing in front of their house

The Brintons often showed magic lantern slides and later films at the Graham Opera House. Frank also managed the Graham Opera House from 1910 to 1917. He often flew models of his airships in the theater during his presentations. While managing the Graham, he built an airdome (open-air theater) in 1908 for summer presentations.

Frank did not get along with his in-laws. At one point, he believed they were poisoning his food. According to the story, he fed some of the suspicious food to the cat, and the cat soon died.

In a letter "to whom it may concern", Frank wrote to prove that he had a great deal of money before his marriage, and that Indiana did little to help earn money. The letter, below, is a transcript of the handwritten letter, unedited, as Frank wrote it. Since he received little formal schooling, the spelling is often phonemic, and the punctuation is non-existent. He also used the old style "f's" where double "s" appeared.

Washington Iowa April 3 1911

To whom it may consern

I the undersigned judging from what has allready been said that in case of my disease (decease?) that my wife and her folks are going to try and make it appear that I wasent worth any thing when I married her and she helped me make all I am worth.

Tharefore I leave thias writings that the trooth may be known When I married my wife I owned in Franklin Township Washington Co I Iowa 162 acres in Lain Co. Kansas I owned 480 acres in Brazoris (Brazos) Co Texas I owned 420 (acres) on this land I was in debt to my mother $3,000.00 to my Aunt Sarah Slagal $1000.00 to the first National Bank $1000.00 making $500000 in all I received of my mother at her death something over $700.00 from my fathers timber land $75.00 making $725.00 leaving a balance of $4225.00 My farm of 160 acres rented for 4 years at $500.00

per year making $2000.00 Two years at $40 per acre each year making in the two years $1280.00 then I then rented it for 4 years at $5.00 per acre for each year making $3200.00 for the 4 years I then rented it for two years at $1000.00 a year which gave me $2000.00 for the two years making in all for rent up to the year 1910 making for rent of one my farms in Franklin Twp Washington Co $8480.00 subtracting the $4225.00 which I owed from what I received for rent leaves me $42255.00 out of this sum I spent about ($3100.00) Thirty one hundred for taxes and improvements leaving a balance of $1155.00 I traded to my Aunt Sara Slagal 160 acres of land in Lain Co Kansas for 80 acres of land in Sec 59 Braforic (Brazoc) Co Texas paying her $400.00 to boot this still leaves me $755.00 which I might of paid out for interest on borrowed money besides my land I had a show that was worth about $1000.00 at the time a married and I had spent a lot of money learning about different places and gathering material for my show which perhaps would add $2000.00 more to the value of the show When I maried my wife she knew nothing about show buinefs and could help me but little in fact she did but little for about 3 years after we was maried She then comenst to do the Booking and helping on the stage by making sounds to accompany the pictures and taking tickets at the door but counting all the time she worked at the Opera House and doing the Booking wouldn't amount to more than four hours a day while I would get up at seven in the morning and work until Eleven at night puting out bills and getting the show ready for night and giving the show at night my expence was heavy as Ive allways stayed at the best hotels taking the best rooms going to and from hotels in bufses to cabs I carried my own Light outfit which cost me about $? One dollar and 75c per day I was continualy buying new picturs and my advertising bills was considerable when we wasent showing we was eather at home Paying our Board to my wifes folks of 50c a piece per day and furnsishing the house and almost all the furniture in which we all lived.

When we wasn't we was travling at a heavy expence going to see the sights boath day and night we attended the Omaha Exposition the Buffalo Expostion the St Louis Exposition two diferent times and the Jamestown Exposition besides we went to visit all most all the Eastern Cities Except Boston Mafs We would often go to Chicago Ill Muscatian Davenort Rock iland Peoria Ill Delavan Ill and Burlington Iowa besides we would Lay of from our show and work and make short Tours goving to Towns of interest at one time in Texas we went on a weeks vacation to Austin and Benantone Texas at other times to Minapolis and St Paul in short we spent all the money we maid in the show busneys in Sight Seeing and the expence of running the show paying hired help buying new films Lantern slides illustrated song slides paying for ? for advance work help telephone meysage telegrams postage newspapers Drayage ? fair buys and Garage hier Hotels londery hall and Opera House rent limes to burn in the Lantern New mushians and Lantern Presents to different peopal money to poor and to Churches and a great many things that a person never thinks save until they are once on the road and in the work in fact all the money are just ahead in the time we was out on the road was ($1600.00) Sixteeen hundred dollars which I paid to Brother Nathan for 160 acres of Land in Sect 59 in Brojoris

(Brazos)County Texas and what money I have in Iowa detals tryin got show where every cent was spent as I never had a 22 thought of it being nefsary to leave any such writings behind and I never dreamed of such a thing until my wife got sick then things began to develop when my wifes father though she was going to die this offend my ? and I thought it best to leave some writings behind that those that was interested might know trooth as I have no desire to leave any thing else behind a serch threw the records will show that my statement is true except an erow I might of made on the account of not keeing a memorandum of every thing but I think by these writing it wll be easy to prove that my wife helped me to lay up but a very small portion of what my property is worth today in fact the advance in the price of the lasnd I had when we was married has maid us more money than anything else. She held me back more than she ever boasted me a head on the account of her lack of buisneyfs ability. I loved my wide and we just got along nicely and I allweys took her with me almost all of my diferent trips and I doent suppse I could of thought of these writings if it hadent of been for my wifes father I kept the in my house for allmost 10 years (?) I let them shift for them selves and ever since that time they have made it very miserable for me and I fully believe after I am gone they will stil continue to use thare influence with my wife to have her look out for no 1 so she can help them W F Brinton

Frank developed pernicious anemia. He made trips to Rochester, Minn. and Iowa City for treatments and often had blood transfusions. He had been ill for two years before his death and was unable to attend to business during that time.

Frank died on December 16, 1919. The Woodford Undertaking took charge of arrangements, and the services.

His funeral was held December 20 at his home at 921 South Iowa. According to funeral records, his bronze casket cost $1,515 and the entire funeral cost $1,770 (about $26,600 in 2020 dollars)·

In his will, he established a trust. Ina would receive income from one third of the trust if she did not remarry. Income from the other two thirds of the trust was to go to non-profit organizations. The Washington County Hospital and Washington YMCA have become primary recipients.

His will stated: "There shall be erected by my estate, a family monument worth not less than One Thousand Dollars, on the lot which my mother Mary Brinton is buried, in Elm Grove Cemetery, and it shall have appropriate inscriptions placed thereon for my mother, my wife and others of the family buried in the same lot."

Brinton
grave
marker in
Elm Grove
cemetery

CHAPTER THREE
INDIANA PUTMAN BRINTON

Indiana Putman, born on December 7, 1877, grew up on a farm, but in a family much less affluent than the Brintons, her future in-laws. She was one of three girls born to Jacob and Ellen Putman. Her family included an older sister Stacie born in 1874, and a younger sister Estie, born in 1886. Estie died at the age of four Stacie and Indiana developed a lifelong rivalry.

Indiana probably attended a one-room school near Verdi and graduated from Washington High School in 1895. While still in high school, she took normal training (teacher education). After graduating, she returned to the Verdi area as a teacher at the Indian Creek

School. She was, by several accounts, well-liked by her students. She taught for only a few terms, perhaps only one.

The Indian Creek School
where Indiana taught

Indiana (top center) with her students at Indian Creek

Indiana married Frank Brinton in Chicago on June 27, 1898. Frank was thirty years her senior.

Brinton
wedding
picture

Indiana became part of the Brinton Entertaining Company but did not perform. "Her job was to sell tickets and look pretty". She became the business manager of the company and was very good at bookkeeping.

The Brintons traveled with their show from Texas to Minnesota, both on their own and with the Chautauqua circuit. They showed much of the central United States audiences their first moving pictures. There were other traveling projectionists, but many considered the Brintons to be the best. Indiana's records show them doing nearly three hundred shows a year from 1902 through 1907. They could draw over one-thousand people to a show in a town with a population of twenty. It was common for them to make $150 a day. They also did programs for county homes and mental hospitals as they traveled.

Indiana flourished with lavish clothes and hats, nice cars, a tastefully appointed home with exotic curios including an Egyptian mummy.

She was extremely protective of Frank during his final illness, telling visitor what topics they could discuss and what was not to be mentioned.

Frank Brinton died on December 16, 1919, after an illness of over a year. His will, dated September 25, 1919, set up a trust to benefit Indiana and the Washington County Hospital.

> The net income from the trust estate as it accrues shall be paid to my wife during life so long as she does not remarry. I desire during this period my wife suitable (sic) and abundantly provided with care, maintenance, comfort and pleasures satisfactory and appropriate to her station. And if her available income at any time becomes inadequate to furnish the same, then the additional funds required therefor may be taken from the principal of the trust estate and be used for such purpose. At the death or remarriage of my wife the whole of the trust estate then remaining shall pass to the Washington County Hospital Association.

Since his will stated that if she remarried, she would be disinherited, she never remarried. She traveled extensively, often

with a "gentleman companion". She also applied for and received additional funds from the trust fund annually.

Indiana continued making wise business choices, especially in land speculation.

She was proud of her complexion and her figure. She had her clothes tailored to fit her figure perfectly, including clothes for her funeral. She had zippers in her dresses along the side rather than the back for a better fit. She would often ask at a drug store, in a loud voice, for feminine products long after it was obvious that she no longer needed them. She had a special recipe for hair coloring, that she kept in her refrigerator and insisted on its use for her funeral. She was a naturalist. Many stories continue to this day, about how she often answered the door wearing only an apron, and at times wore it backwards.

On the reverse of this photograph, Indiana wrote "There are those who say I am corseted, but I am not"

Indiana later used the name "Ina" instead of Indiana, even later she used the name Diana.

She traveled extensively and often wintered in Texas or Florida. She visited the Pan-American Exposition in Buffalo, New York in 1901.

Indiana and her mother
while visiting Mexico

While she was wintering in Miami, she attended a rally for Franklin Roosevelt, on February 15, 1933, when an assassin attempted to shoot the president elect. Before the event began, Ina changed seats to get a better view. Mrs. Joseph Gill took the seat Indiana vacated. One of the eight people shot that day was Mrs. Gill.

In an article for the *Washington Evening Journal* on July 2, 1947, Indiana stated she preferred traveling by bus for trips shorter than 1,000 miles. She said that bus stations were much more convenient than railroad stations.

She lived in mainly in Texas and maintained the house in Washington using it more as an office than home when she had business matters in the area.

Her sister Stacie Putnam Powelson had a long-standing jealousy of Ina. Shortly after Frank and Indian built their new house, Stacie had her husband build a house that had to be one inch larger in every direction than her sister's house. Shortly after finishing the house, Mr. Powelson drove to Muscatine, where he walked into the Mississippi River and drowned.

After Indiana's funeral service, Stacie kicked the casket and broke her toe.

Indiana died on May 23, 1955 in Rochester, Minnesota where she had been receiving treatment at the Mayo Clinic. She had the most expensive funeral in the history of the county. She pre-selected a solid, bronze sarcophagus that was too heavy for the Jones Funeral Home's hearse. It took equipment borrowed from the utility company to lower it into her grave. The epitaph on the Brinton grave marker is "They have fallen."

Police reported thieves entered the house April 14, 1956, but no report is available on anything taken. Her Executors held sale of household items from the estate on September 26, 1957.

Ina's final will, dated March 30, 1942, established the Frank and Indiana Trust to establish:

A charitable, education and Christian organization to receive benefits under this will shall specialize in the building of character and in assisting individuals to better understand themselves and each other as well to understand life's purpose. My desire is to assist toward the attainment of life – 100% viz, the purpose of Creation.

Through the years, the trust has given significant money to the YMCA and the Washington Community Hospital as well as many other charitable entities. The trust still exists, and each year continues to support non-profit organizations.

CHAPTER FOUR
THE BRINTON ENTERTAINMENT COMPANY

Frank Brinton entered the entertainment business when he gave his first magic lantern presentation in West Chester, Iowa in 1879.

A "magic lantern" projected images on to a screen through a lens with a light source using transparent plates, usually made of glass. Brinton accompanied his slide show with lectures, music and displays of costumes and artifacts from the Holy Land. Frank took many of his slides while he was living in Egypt.

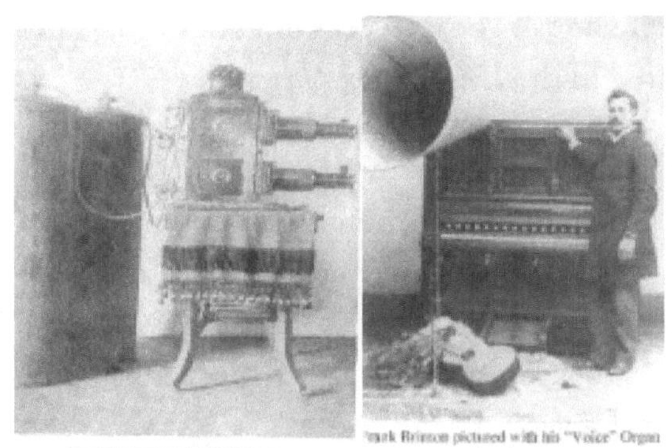

Frank Brinton pictured with his "Voice" Organ

Brinton's Acetylene Powered Projector

He used a Stereopticon projector. This did not project images in three-dimensions but allowed him to dissolve from one slide to another. In addition to slides of the Holy Land, he had a variety of scenic, sing-along

music and humorous slides. Some of his slides had hand-cranked moving backgrounds that gave the appearance of movement on the screen. This gave a waterfall or fountain the illusion of moving water. Other slides showed fire in a building or smoke coming from a steam ship.

Frank Brinton formed the Brinton Entertaining Company in 1882. He gave his first performance in West Chester, Iowa. In December, he gave three different performances at Everson's Opera House in Washington, Iowa. Admission was 10 cents and 20 cents with all three nights for 45cents. He had shown previously for six weeks in Des Moines, and had several testimonials printed in the *Washington Gazette*.

> It gives me great pleasure to recommend W. F. Brinton's Stereopticon entertainment of any church society wishing to get up in anything of the kind, I have attended six and was instructed and entertained, by his views of Palestine especially. His entertainments are all of a decidedly religious turn and will do good wherever given

Rev. W. M. Bartholomew, Pastor East Des Moines Church.
A review in the May 29, 1883, issue of the *Washington Press* stated:

> There were not so many people "on the interior" of the Graham at Brinton's picture lectures as there should have been, considering their merits. Was not the music on the steamboats entrancing? Has not the little man on the table a singing voice like a very young robin's? There were some new views. The mummified cadaver of Ramses was 'a bute,' and many of the scenery views were 'grand beyond description.'

Mr. Brinton stands well in front of commentator. But he was way off in saying that St. Peter was ever in Rome. The scholars prove he was never there even half a minute. People rallied for the part fountain. The 2d night very good house, and Brinton said he would throw in all the receipts Monday night.

Brinton often gave part of the receipts to various projects. Part of the May 29 receipts went to Washington's park improvement fund.

The *Washington Evening Journal* reviewed an 1897 performance at the Graham Opera House in Washington.

Pictures that Move and Ships that Fly – W.F. Brinton opened a three nights' engagement at the Graham Opera House last night. He has quite a combination for a single evening's entertainment. The program last evening was put on for the first time. Few from the county and out of town were present. His two ships were suspended and allowed to propel themselves in a circle on the stage.

He clearly demonstrates his theory of propelling and navigating the air.

The fore part of the program consisted of some lantern views and scenes collected during Mr. Brinton's trip abroad.

Miss Josie Britton recited, and vocal solos were rendered by master Raven Harmon and Miss Blanch Britton. Miss Birdie Craven rendered a piano solo and furnished music while many of the pictures were exhibited. An entire change of program was announced for tonight. An excursion will be run up from Winfield to accommodate the people along the Narrow-Gauge line.

The "pictures that move" referred to the mechanical magic lantern slides, not moving pictures. Birdie Craven, the pianist, later became an actress and appeared in New York City in Charles's Frohman's company which was a noted theatrical company of the time.

When moving pictures became available, Brinton was one of the first to present them.

Frank Brinton first showed motion pictures there as part of the 4th of July celebrations and again on July 15 and 16, 1898. His films included *the Battle of Manila, the Landing of the Troops near Santiago, the Boys Marching to the Front* and *the Bombardment of Matanzas* (during the Spanish-American War). Admission was 10 cents, 15 cents and 25 cents. One-fourth of the receipts went to the boys who left Washington County and were then in the army.

Brinton was not the first to show moving pictures at the Graham. On Thursday, May 13, 1897, someone showed Edison's Kinetoscope films there. The Graham Opera House, renamed the State Theater, is still showing films. In 2016, the Guinness Book of World's Records designated it as the "Longest continuously operating cinema in the World".

Other early film showings included, on October 20, 21, 22, 1898, The Ideal Specialty Company showing Cineograpic films and a Hindu magician specializing in snakes.

In July 1898, the *Washington Gazette* reported:

W.F. Brinton returned Tuesday evening from Chicago, where he has been gathering some of the finest Spanish and American war pictures that are now in existence. . . Brinton got many others some costing as much as $30.00 apiece. On Saturday evening July 15th he will give his first exhibition of these new scenes in the Graham Theater. Admission 10c, 15c and 20c. One-fourth of the receipts goes to the boys who left Washington County and are now in the army. A naval combat was never photographed before; but this was done at an enormous expense, therefore you can sit in a comfortable seat here at home and see the ships in real action, with life-like motion so natural that you can almost imagine that you hear the cannon's roar and smell the powder.

February 3, 1899, *Washington Evening Journal:*

W.F. Brinton has just made an estimation of the number of pictures he has for the kinescope. They number 24,600 pictures. When place on a strip of celluloid one against the other they measure almost one-half mile in length. There will be s strip of these pictures shown tonight that measure over one-fourth of a mile. These will be interspersed with music from the Donovan orchestra.

Frank Brinton with his film
projector in the
Graham Opera House

The *Washington Evening Journal* reported on June 8, 1904:
W. F. Brinton appeared at the

Graham last evening for the fiftieth time, the entertainment being under the auspices of the Woman's Relief Corps. Mr. Brinton always has he crowd, but last evening the crowd was extraordinarily large, owing partly to the efforts of the society for whose benefit it was given. His pictures varied last evening. He has his famous train robbery pictures Buffalo Bill's show, etc. His set of comic views and some of his scenes of the Holy Land. The male quartet sang a number of songs, which were illustrated, among them being "Always in the way." "Star Spangled Banner," "Way down upon the

Suwanee River," etc. The entire evening was one that was pleasing,

entertaining and interesting. Quite a neat sum was realized, all of which is to go toward the relief of the poor of the community.

Poster for the Brinton Entertaining Company

Brinton took his show on the road. The 1904 Route book contains much information about the Brinton Entertaining Company of that year. It gives the date of the performance, the name of the town and the income received. Sometimes, it gave the percentage of the sales received, and occasionally the weather. Performers at this

time usually worked for a percentage of the ticket sales, sometimes with a minimum amount guaranteed, the balance went to the venue. The back of the route book contains the names of hotels in which they strayed in each town.

In 1904, The Brintons gave 184 performances. They earned $8,687.17. (This would be almost $261,233 in 2023 dollars). Their percentage of the ticket sales ranged from twenty to fifty percent. There largest take was $117.30 in Winona, Minnesota; and the smallest was $4.95 in West Branch, Iowa. (Three larger amounts are listed for Washington, Iowa, however they may be for combined performances). They gave ten performances in their "new" tent.

The towns they played in 1904 in Iowa were: Ainsworth, Anamosa, Blairstown, Brighton, Brooklyn, Cascade, Central City, Charles City, Clarion, Crawfordsville, Eagle Grove, Eddyville, Fremont, Grinnell, Hampton, Hedrick, Independence, Iowa City, Kalona, Keota, Keswick, Malcom, Manchester, Marshalltown, Martinsburg, Mason City, Monticello, Montezuma, Mount Pleasant, North English, Norway, Ollie, Richland, Sheffield, Sigourney, Tipton, Washington, Waterloo, Waverly, Wayland, Webster, Wellman, West Branch, West Chester, What Cheer, Williamsburg.

In Minnesota they performed in: Chesterfield, Faribault, Mankato, New Ulm, Owatonna, Rochester, Saint Charles, Saint Peter, Waseta, Waterville, Wells, Winona.

They took time off twice to attend the St. Louis World's Fair.

The 1905 Route Book gives similar information. They gave 230 performances in 65 Iowa towns, 12 in Minnesota, 9 in Nebraska and 2 in Kansas. Their income was

$12,667.40 ($371,000 in 2023 dollars).

From 1910 until 1917, Brinton rented and

was manager of the Graham Opera House in Washington, Iowa. While manager he supervised a major redecoration costing over $1,000 of his own money (over $27,000 in 2023 dollars).

The Graham Opera House in Washington, Iowa

THE AIRDOME

Airdomes became popular in the early twentieth century as a summer alternative to opera houses before the advent of air conditioning. They were open-air amphitheaters surrounded by walls.

Frank Brinton erected his airdome in the summer of 1908. He located it on a sloping lot, one block south of the square at 216-218 South Iowa. The structure had a concrete orchestra pit, and the raised seating had a sand floor. Seating capacity was 800. Concession booths near the entrance provided both food and drinks.

Brinton' Airdome

It opened June 6, 1908. Over 1,000 attended and many others turned away. Admission prices were 5 cents for ground seats and 10 cents for elevated seating. Brinton paid the city a twenty-five-dollar license fee and rented the ground for one-hundred dollars each year.

The airdome presented a variety of entertainments, like those presented in the opera house. Popular presentations included plays, moving pictures, vaudeville acts, wrestling competitions.

The list of films shown on August 6, 1908 included The *Dream of an Opium Fiend, Stage Memories of an Old Theatrical Troupe, The Younger Brother Clover Blossoms* and *A Tear, a Kiss, a Smile.*

The advertisement for the June 15, 1908, performance listed:
At the Airdome

The story of "Alibaba" in hand colored moving pictures at the airdome tonight, introducing oriental custom, decorations and drills with gorgeous colorings. Explanation of the story give. In addition, there will be a great variety of new moving pictures including many ludicrous situations and two illustrated songs. Everything new, program lasts one hour and a half. Lower floor 5 cents,

elevated seats 10 cents. Band and orchestra music each evening. The time of performance at the airdome hereafter for all evenings except Saturday will be at 8 o'clock. Doors will open at 7:30.

An article in the June 26, 1908, issue of the *Washington Evening Journal* stated:
Large Crowd Witnessed "the Burning

of Rome "at the Airdome

The popularity of the airdome is still increasing, and last night it was almost taxed to its capacity, the great feature, "NERO AND THE BURNING OF ROME" being presented. This was a high class historic and religious production, instructive as well as entertaining,

combining the great events, life and customs of Rome at that age and the burning of the Eternal City with a thrilling love story founded on the persecution of the Christians, introducing throughout the play grand historical sites, including the feast of Diana, Nero in his palace with his dancing maidens offering incense on the altar of Diana the persecution and imprisonment of the Christians, the arena, gladiator combats, dungeons under the Coliseum, Christian and Pagan worship and varieties of historical events, the play closing with a good finish with the hero and heroine of the story united, the accepting the faith and the cross while the vision of angels appears in the smoke of burning Rome. It is a magnificent production and contains such a diversity of interest that all can be pleased. Explanation was given in detail so that even the children could understand, which added greatly to the interest and pleasure. This is a new moving picture just out, and it was with difficulty that the airdome could secure it at such an early date, the demand for it being so great. In addition to this feature a variety of other interesting subjects were presented, one highly colored magic production with gorgeous costumes and drill being especially meritorious, while the typical presentation of everyday life in Holland with the Holland windmills and two-wheel carts proved a pleasing sight to all.

The program was enlivened with comedy, and the band and orchestra added effects to the scenes which were highly appreciative. The illustrated songs were well rendered and popular with the audience. With such a high-class program at such cheap prices in a cool and delightful place of amusement, it is not strange that the popularity of the airdome is increasing. Same program tonight. Entire change program tomorrow night.

The pictures used at the air dome at all times are the first grade from the highest priced manufactured in the business. Nothing cheap used. The airdome is built for a high class place of amusement for refined people; the same rules observed as in an opera house. Full evening's entertainment each night. Lower floor, 5 cents, elevated seats, 10 cents. Elevated seats cheked (sic).

Brinton made improvements for the 1909 season. On May 15, the *Washington Evening Journal* reported,

"The raised seats will be covered, rain or shine."

It is assumed this was done by a tent like canvass top. Brinton offered to allow special groups use it free of charge including old soldiers organizations, the Ladies Relief Corps and churches for Sunday evening services. The 1909 season closed on September 9.

In 1910, prices raised to 10 cents and 15 cents. The last advertisement for what would be the last program presented at the airdome appeared on September 3, 1910. The airdome closed Sept 24, 1910 and never reopened. No reason for the permanent closing appeared.

In an advertisement on December 16, 1910, Brinton said "having sold my airdome, I wish to sell my electric plant."

Brinton gave up his lease of the Graham Opera House in 1917 and retired from the entertainment business due to ill health.

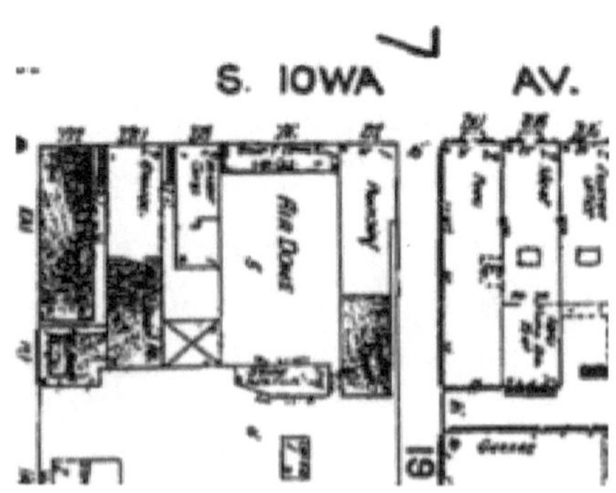

**1909 Sanborn Insurance Map showing
the Airdome**

CHAPTER FIVE
BRINTON'S AIRSHIPS

The first mention of Frank Brinton's interest in flying machines was in his mother's Journal of 1890. An entry stated, "Frank is out working on his airship again."

The *Washington Evening Journal* reported on August 11, 1896:

Brinton's Air Ship

Mr. Brinton is still laboring faithfully on his air ship near Grace Hill. He has just received a 5 horsepower gasoline engine for a small one he is building. When all is completed, he intends to sail into Washington. It will be advertised, and a large crowd will be present to see it operate.

He worked with a powered movable wing, trying to copy the wing strokes of a bird. He first used one 12' x 6' wing, then went to four 12' x 6' wings moved by a gasoline powered steam engine. The craft would move across land but did not go into the air. Brinton then worked with "fixed wing" craft.

Photo of one of Brinton's airships, the label is in his handwriting.

As the Brintons traveled doing their projected entertainment programs, Frank had a propeller-driven craft tethered to a pole in their tent. No known photographs show this, but accounts and Brinton's own writings mention it. He also flew models of various airships in the Graham Opera House, in Washington, Iowa.

Local people made fun of Frank's flight experiments. He reluctantly agreed to hold a public exhibition of his latest craft on September 20, 1899. The airship had a large cigar-shaped dirigible to enable vertical ascensions and landing. Frank and Indiana had built their home on South Iowa Avenue with a landing space on top for such airships.

He decided to convince the public of the genuineness of his theory he must build a large aircraft, and he went to work and built a large balloon cigar shape. Over this he placed a net to give it strength, and this net was made fast to the mechanical power, and steering apparatus that swung beneath. This sort of work was entirely new to Brinton, and he tried to secure competent help, but none were available.

He had no generator for the manufacture of gas for the dirigible and ordered one from a firm in Des Moines who promised to supply him with the desired generator several days in advance of his exhibition.

The "Ascension Day" came. Banks closed, and schools dismissed. Thousands of people came to Washington to the fairgrounds to watch. They paid twenty-five cents to see the first manned flight. The part needed for the hydrogen generator did not arrive.

The morning of the exhibition he received the freight bill which was given to him by Mr. Fred Stewart, of Washington, who said he had just received the bill, and the generator was up at the station. Brinton hurried down to the fairground to make necessary arrangements, leaving orders for the generator to be rushed down with all speed.

It was an ideal day and people came by the thousands, and the fairground had several kinds and entertainment such as is often seen at fairs, and everything was made ready as nearly as possible for the promised exhibition, but to Brinton's surprise and apparent defeat he received word that the generator was not at the station. What to do. Brinton did not know, as the fairground was partly filled with people who had paid an admission of 25c had got too far to be stopped at that time.

Brinton thinking if possible to inflate the balloon with tight empty barrels properly joined together, he sent up into the city and gathered a load, joining them as quickly as possible and making a certain mixture to generate the gas he set to going, but as the time was growing short he hurried the chemical action which caused it to ferment and the steam that rose form the mixing gas carried with it a certain amount of sulphuric acid, which caused the balloon cloth to decay to a certain extent, but no holes were eaten through the cloth. He went on and did everything in his power to inflate the balloon.

Many of his friends trying to assist him got sulphuric acid on their clothes, which soon rendered them useless as a Sunday suit, which Brinton replaced, buying each one a new suit. Brinton saw that to inflate the balloon with this kind of an apparatus was impossible, and he caused the mechanical part of the apparatus to be run into the fair ground, where he mounted it and tried to explain the cause of his failure and to show and tell the people how the apparatus would perform if properly equipped. At this time Brinton stated that he thinks that he saw more angry people when he announced that the apparatus would not go. Some rough necks who saw a little chance for some fun grabbed the tongue of the wagon on which the aircraft was place and tried to run with it, but one of Brinton's men seeing their object, grabbed the pole that was lying nearby and shoved it through the spokes of the back wheels, thus depriving them of their pleasure.

Some men trampled upon the balloon, dropping lighted cigars, trying to set it on fire. Some had kodaks, who came prepared for photographing, commenced their work. Others trying to brush back the crowd, told them to make room for the photographers that they might get some photographs of the biggest fakir that ever lived, and comical remarks were heard here and there.

A photo taken on "Ascension Day", September 20, 1899

Two men, while walking through the crowds. One stretched himself up and said to the other, "What in h-—is Frank trying to do anyway? The other said: "Don't you see the large net; he is fishing for suckers." The other man said: "Well he certainly got a good mess of them today."

One of the prominent ministers of the city went asked him to give him back his quarter, as he paid it in good faith believing that he would see the advertised exhibition but he had really seen nothing, as he did not care for races, later when Brinton was told this by the gate keeper, he told him to tell this minister the next time he saw him not to worry about the quarter, for he had apparently received no more benefit than those who attended the air ship exhibition but added that perhaps the fault was in himself.

It appeared that almost every person on the fairground was mad at the announcement at the air ship failure. Some of the more bold and vicious men rushed up to Brinton and demanded that he pay them their money back, but he was unable to so do as the money taken in had long since been carried to the bank and was locked up in the vault, but he happened to have a few quarters in his pocket which he took out and started in to satisfy the demands of the men. Others of his friends rushed in and told him that he should not pay to these men another cent, as they had already received their money's worth for the attractions that had been pulled off during the day. These attractions were races of different kinds made to go the best three out of five.

Two brass bands were playing most of the time to entertain the people. The men who were receiving their money back got very angry at Mr. Brinton's friends who interfered with their receiving their money back as they believed that Mr. Brinton would have continued to have paid back the money if left alone, but this of course he could not do.

A man who had taken his family early in the morning and driven 20 miles and paid their admission into the fair ground, was returning home that night when met by a relative of his who wanted to hear about the air ship exhibition, as he could not attend on the account of other business. To this request the man with the family said that Mr. Brinton had met with great success, but when he was able to get up in the air, he lost control of his machine, and the last thing they saw of Mr. Brinton and his craft he was down over the city of Muscatine going like h-—and was in danger of being drowned in the Mississippi.

This, of course aroused his relative's curiosity who wanted to know more. Finally, he was told that, I will now give you the truth. "The last time I saw of the air ship was the balloon was stretched out upon the fairground like any other old dirty rag, and there was a possibility of a mob being formed to take care of Mr. Brinton."

Sometime before Brinton arranged for the exhibition, he engaged the opera house to give a show that night. When he found out he had disappointed the people at the fairgrounds he agreed to let all into the opera house that could get in free of charge. His show outfit was then taken to the opera house and again to his surprise the opera house officials would not allow him to occupy the opera house, saying that the people were worked up and to such an extent that they would probably tear the show outfit in pieces, and would probably destroy the opera house.

Failing in getting the opera house, he then secured the side of a large store building

and was making arrangements to give his show there, but the officials of the city sent the sheriff to Brinton telling him that he would have to abandon this plan, which he did, sending his show outfit home. Brinton then started to walk along the east side of the square, when he was met by the clerk form the Colenso Hotel, who told him there was a gentleman at the hotel who wanted to see him. He accompanied the clerk to the hotel where he met one of the official of the W. R. R. Co. who introduced himself, telling Brinton that he had come to hire him to take his air ship in two weeks to the Oskaloosa fair grounds and there give an exhibition but Brinton quickly told him that would be impossible as he had failed in his exhibition here at Washington and he would not undertake another so soon. Then the gentleman said he was very sorry to hear, as he had been busily engaged in arranging for the excursions to the Oskaloosa fair grounds, and that day he and the fairgrounds company had made arrangement for a place from which the air ship would start on its flight, But Brinton told him that he was very sorry to disappoint him, but that would have to be the case at this time.

While in this conversation continued a good friend of Brinton's followed him into the interior of another room in the hotel. This friend requested him to get a bed and remain in the hotel that night for he felt that he would be in great danger if he undertook to go home that night. To this Brinton made the reply that he had no fear of the people, and his wife would be expecting him home and he would have to go.

This friend told Brinton that he felt sure that he was honest in what he had undertaken, and for that reason he felt it his duty to warn him of the danger and save him from what he considered a hazardous undertaking but failing in getting him to consent to stay in the hotel he left and went out among the people. During this time Mr. Brinton's wife had been hunting for him and hearing that he was at the hotel she went in and found him. There she was introduced to the official of the N. W. R Co. and a general conversation followed on the present day's experience.

Presently back came his friend but calling him to the door told him that he had been out among the crowd, and he found many of the had been drinking to a certain extent, and he wanted to warn him in the danger in trying go home and told him to take his advice and get a bed and stay. This he did not and ordered his bed, not when the officials of the hotel learned of the excitement, they changed the number of the room that Mr. and Mrs. Brinton were to occupy, thinking that if the mob entered by force they would have some trouble in finding where these two guests were located. Soon the crowd began to disburse and before long, there were only a few folks left on the square, and it was not long until Washington was enjoying a peaceful rest.

Brinton did not sleep much that night and was up early the next morning. After breakfast, the made his way to the Journal

office, which was published at that time by Mr. Payne. The editor was apparently much out of humor and gave Brinton a "jacking up" for the disappointment he gave the people the previous day. The editor was assisted by another prominent citizen of Washington, who joined to make it as uncomfortable for Brinton as possible.

That evening he ran a long article in the evening paper stating that if the people of Washington had not had a heavy frost that night it was not because a hard chill had been thrown about the town.

Brinton also put in an article of his own which fully explained to the people the cause of his failure and other comments and articles were published in nearly all the papers of the county principally ng his efforts. criticized This was perhaps as much as an ad and more so than if there had been a straight flight with the air ship.

The following paragraph appeared in *The Washington Evening Journal* article but not in *The Washington Democrat:*

> One of the Oskaloosa papers had the comment which read like this; Washington is a little town down on the Rock Island on the other side of Keota, where they build air ships that never fly, train blood hounds to chase their fellowmen and imprison editors for publishing the news. At that time the sheriff of Washington had some hounds training, and the editor of *The Brighton Enterprise* was serving a term in the Washington County jail for publishing an article to the discredit of a Brighton citizen.

The next evening after the air ship failure, Mr. Brinton was looking through his mail and found a letter which contained these words" "The committee advise you to leave. Had we gotten you last night you would never have stolen any more money. The committee will keep an eye on you." This was accompanied by the skull and cross bones, and somewhat aroused Brinton's feelings, therefore thinking that the excitement was not yet over, he armed himself and his two hired men and awaited results. For the good of all the nigh passed off very quietly and this apparently ended all excitement.

After meeting with the failure at the fairgrounds he put forth and effort of get others interested with him in making long trips to other cities to interest men who had had more practical experience in the balloon business. At one time, he made a trip to see some noted balloonists, and to tell them of his theory, and if possible, to get them to go into partnership with him, and they would build a large aircraft to experiment work, but this was met with a flat refusal.

These noted men told him his theory was certainly groundless, and such an aircraft would prove a failure, but the leading man who had listened carefully to Brinton's claims took care to call his partner and have Brinton rehearse his claims, and they succeeded in making Brinton feel a little discouraged in his invention. Some had kodaks, who came prepared for photographing, commenced their work.

Others trying to brush back the crowd, told them to make room for the photographers that they might get some photographs of the biggest fakir that ever lived, and comical remarks were heard here and there.

People certainly had great faith in Mr. Brinton as an inventor for this they were knew was his first attempt on a large scale. Along this line, but however their faith was so strong that court being in session all were dismissed, and they came to the fair ground

gentleman said he was very sorry to hear, as he had been busily engaged in arranging for the excursions to the Oskaloosa fair grounds, and that day he and the fairgrounds company had made arrangement for a place from which the air ship would start on its flight,

Some people were upset, and the Brintons were secreted from town to nearby Ainsworth for their safety. For the rest of his career, Frank always gave free admission to his show to anyone who said that they had been to Ascension Day. Brinton continued to work with flight for the rest of his life but had no more big public flight exhibitions.

Frank with a model of one of his airships.

Brinton went to Washington D. C. to talk with President McKinley about his airships. He wanted to invite the president to Washington, Iowa to take a ride, but was unable to visit with the President.

Brinton promoted the total safety of his airship. He built his last model to carry twelve passengers. He also felt there was great potential for military uses for his "Practical Air Ship." In some of his final writings, Frank was still talking of flight and his regret of not flying.

After reviewing plans and drawings, engineers at the University of Iowa believe that some of Brinton's airships would have flown. Had the airship flown on Ascension Day, it would have been four years before the wright Brothers' famous flight.

Two models of Brinton's airships

The Washington Evening Journal of January 23, 1917, reported:

BRINTON HAS NEW MODEL OF AIRSHIP WILL OFFER NEW IDEAS IN AREOPHANE CONSTRUCTION TO GOVERNMENT.

W.F. Brinton is engaged in perfecting a model for an airship of his design and construction. Less than two weeks ago he began work on his model, after having he ideas for the craft clearly outlined in his mind, and yesterday evening show repre-sentatives of the Journal the almost

almost completed model. A few minor parts are yet to be fitted and then the miniature areophane will be sent to Washington D. C. and an offer for its sale made to the government for war purposes.

Several new ideas are embraced in Mr. Brinton's plans of this machine, which he confidently believes will revolutionize travel through the air. The body of the craft is built in curves, there being no square corners in the construction. The framework will be of some light material, probably of aluminum, of an oval shape, and supported underneath with three boats, in which will be the engines, steering and controlling apparatus and passengers. It is to be a hydroplane, capable of traveling in the air, on the water or on the land.

One novel idea that Mr. Brinton intends to incorporate in the airship will be a contrivance that will enable it to move backward as well as forward. It will have three sets of propellers on each end, as well as two on each side. It will have places for four engines, and its inventor believes that it will be so equipped as to guarantee against every element of danger through accident. But the most novel idea of all is a parachute contrivance which can be used in case the machine is disabled land which a landing can be made safely Mr. Brinton believes.

The model is made of tin, steel rods and wire and is a neat little affair. Mr. Brinton does not intend to at this time make a machine of working size but will present is ideas in the form of a model to the war department and see what the army people who are experts in such things, think of his suggestions. He plans to have his ideas patented. Mr. Brinton yesterday evening said he believes they could not be as the flying ability of an airship contrived along the lines he suggests in his model, for he has done his work carefully and believes his ship is designed on correct principles. It has numerous new elements in its manufacture, which appeal to one as substantial improvement over any airship now in use.

Twenty years ago, Mr. Brinton began his experiments with airships and has been tremendously interested in them ever since, although not having time or opportunity to work out his ideas as he would have wished. He has followed closely the developments in air travel and is in a position to know "what is what" on the subject. Seventeen years ago, he perfected a machine which failed to work only because of the non-arrival of necessary parts. The present model is built along modern lines and has numerous improvements, which Mr. Brinton believes will make it the best thing yet suggested in aerial inventions.

The principle features of this new model was shown in the mechanical part of his airship, which he tried to fly at the fairgrounds September 29, 1889.

The following detailed article appeared in the *Washington Democrat* on September 24, 1919. The same article appeared in the September 27 issue of the *Washington Evening Journal*, with some minor modifications. These appeared just three months before Frank's death. No author was credited in either article, it is possible that Frank wrote it himself using the third person perspective.

Washington's First Aerial Navigation Agitator

W. F. Brinton, of Washington, Iowa, Asks Permission for Space, Among the Early Pioneers and Adventures of Aerial Navigation. He also Believes that Advocates Asking this Privilege Should Give Proof Showing Their Worthiness of Such Claims.

In the latter part of 1890, Mr. Brinton discovered the theory of the possibilities of navigating the air and spent some time in talking this theory to others, often taking with him prominent men to his private room, and there explaining to them his theories, but he was generally met with remarks saying that it was something they had never thought on and were unprepared to give advice. Mr. Brinton told them that he had strong faith in his theory, but if they say anything that looked unreasonable or impossible, he wished that they would be free to make mention of it, for he would likely spend a lot of time and money on the invention. He often spent lots of time in thinking and planning for motor power and wondering how this might be gained. He made but little effort this line until the summer of 1892. This time he was making his home with his renter on the farm. It was in the summer of 1893. His first plan was to get a satisfactory motor power. He purchased first a small steam engine heated by gasoline. This engine he arranged with gear wheels to drive a wing power at a certain speed. He only tried to the proper working of one wing at first. This wing measured 12 feet in length and 6 feet in width but being so large of course could not be handled very rapidly. He experimented with this for some little time in changing the different strokes trying to imitate that of a bird. One day he had been experimenting during the forenoon and his renter came in from the field and Mr. Brinton called his attention to see this wing work. During the forenoon, a chain belt had been giving him some trouble, and he asked Thos. Schilling, his renter, if he

would not please take a stick that was lying close by and hold the chain on the pulley. This Mr. Schilling willingly tried to do, but in holding the chain belt he got is hand in the way of the arm of the wing and when it came around it got him by the neck and pressed him over pretty close to the body of the machine, which made his eyes stick out a little farther than normal, as he did not know how close it would come before it would let up, but presently it released its pressure and went on completing the stroke. As soon as Mr. Schilling was released, he stepped back and said that was all the experience he wanted of that kind. This completed Mr. Brinton's experimenting with the one wing system.

He then made a trip to his hometown, Washington, Iowa, seven miles in distance, and there he purchased four large sulky wheels which he placed upon their axles, suing them to carry the aircraft instead of the balloon building a trench from his barn, but through his orchard.

This aircraft had four large wings, the same size of the one just described; but all were made to operate in unison and were driven by the same engine that was used for the first wing. The heating power was gasoline. Mr. Brinton would light the gasoline and as soon as the speed had risen to about 80lb. pressure he would then jump on the machine, turn on the steam and ride as through the orchard as the steam would carry him, the air craft was pushed by hand back to the starting point, As Mr. Brinton did not wish to spend more money in the reversing of the steam power. One day he had done a lot of experimenting in running his machine out and then pushing it back to the starting point, he would make certain changes as he thought was necessary as an improvement. About dusk, Mr. Schilling and his hired man came in from the cornfield where they had been husking corn. And Mr. Brinton, being a little proud of his success that day, called to them to come see his machine work, but he wising to show it up in a little extra style, let the steam run up to 1000 lbs. then jumping on the air craft and turning on a full head of steam the machine lunged forward with apparently more determination to fly than ever before, but it had not run but a short distance until a small pinon broke. This released the entire power to a fraction of nothing, and the engine ran as fast as the steam could drive it, which includes quite a roaring noise as the steam struck the gasoline flame that heated the steam and blew it back for some little distance. It being somewhat dark caused the flame to shine out quite brightly. Mr. Brinton knew at a moment what had happened and sprang forward to shut off the steam. When Mr. Schilling and his hired man saw Mr. Brinton make the sudden spring and hearing the noise, they thought it time for them to be going and started for the opposite side of the barn as soon as Mr. Brinton got the steam shut off he went to see what had become of his guests, and going to the opposite side of the barn he saw them both standing listening for results. Mr. Brinton asked them what was their hurry for getting to the opposite side of the barn, Mr. Shilling said that steam power was something that he did not know anything about, and when he saw Mr. Brinton make the sudden spring he thought he would be going, but he said he never realized before that it was such a distance to the opposite side of the barn. This ended Mr. Brinton's experimenting with the steam power, as it was entirely too heavy for any flights.

After this he experimented of a certain extent upon aerial navigation by areophane, but this he suddenly abandoned as he could not get light enough engine, and he considered even if it should be obtained that it would probably cost the life of many people. This was some time in advance of the Wright Bros. success. At another time he hired a large Chautauqua canvas and crew to

pitch and care for the same and they traveled from town to town stopping one night in a place. At one end of the tent, he had levers fastened to a center pole which extended out for some distance. Then he caused to carry the mechanical part of his airship instead of gas balloons. These were driven by gasoline engines which caused the propellers to beat rapidly upon the air, and in these he caused men to ride, and as the propellers struck the air the mechanical part was driven around the center pole with great rapidity, thus proving again that the propellers had great pulling power. Mr. Brinton was continually working upon different kinds of models, which were often made mention of the in the county and daily papers, and a tinner by the name of Al Roe, who is still in business in Washington, has work upon a number of them.

After a time, he concluded that the dirigible balloons built in cigar shape and covered with a net which could be made fast by a mechanical power swung beneath would be the most successful aircraft that could be built. He first made two small balloons about one foot in diameter and two and one-half feet in length cigar shape. These he varnished and made as nearly airtight as he could possibly make them. The motor power swung beneath was made of coil springs and wound up with a key. These were tied to each end of a long scantling which had a rope tied in the middle, and then fastened up in the scenery loft of the opera house, where he often gave exhibitions. He would at first give some sort of entertainment, then he would lecture upon his theory of navigating the air, presenting the models and telling the people about their possibilities, describing how distance could be shortened by the cutoff that the aircraft could make so claiming that the aircraft in time bridge the Atlantic Ocean. At the close of his lecture, he would release the friction that had held the spring power and then these caused the propellers swung below the balloon to beat upon the air, and in a short time they were going at quite a speed traveling in a circle around the stage, being carried by the scantling instead of inflated gas balloons. This the public looked on and listened to with a great deal of interest to the claims that Brinton made for their success.

He traveled from city to city carrying with him a stereopticon that he used to present in his entertainments showing the places he had visited when traveling through the foreign eastern countries presenting the most of them at Jerusalem and Palestine where he had lived off and on for a period of between two and three years, proving to the people that the Bible was a true book, and everything that he found in Palestine went to confirm the truth of the Bible.

He would stop in one city three nights in the best opera house he could get, charging a small admission for those who wished to attend, but at the close of each exhibition he brought forth his aircraft models and gave exhibitions with them which were apparently looked upon with a great deal of interest, but it was something entirely new to the people, they did not seem to grasp the full meaning of this machine. In the next town, and his wife who traveled with him, would spend four nights, exhibiting three nights and resting over Sunday. These tours were very extensive, traveling from east to west and from north to south, going as far south as the Gulf of Mexico. Such a tour was really a school given the public along the promotion of aerial navigation.

These flights being among the first were largely advertised in the different papers of the w and did a great deal to promote aerial navigation the 20 years or more that Mr. Brinton advocated it with such earnestness that in a short time he got the crank name of "Air Ship Brinton" and they apparently knew at once who they meant, for all Brinton had had for many reverses and had met with so much opposition it is a wonder that he ever stood up against the terrible strain, but his mind is apparently as clear as ever and he still advocates the possibility of navigating the air, and claims that serial navigation will prove in time the greatest invention in the world.

After meeting with his failure at the fairgrounds he published an article in the *Washington Evening Journal* telling the cause of his apparent failure. Nearly every paper in the country had some comment on the failure, and thousands upon thousands read them with interest, and Brinton believes that such failures did more to promote navigation than if he had made successful flights through the air. One morning after he had published the article about his airship failure, he met with Dr. McClain, a prominent doctor of Washington at the time, who said to Mr. Brinton; "I thank you for publishing that article, for I believe it to be true, as I know your people better than you do." He said he knew them for four generations. He knew Mr. Brinton and family, his father and family, his grandfather and family, and his great grandfather and family, and they were all truthful people.

CHAPTER SIX
AFTERWARD

Indiana was a wise businesswoman. She bought property around the country and was a major investor in the Iowa Colony development in Texas.

When Indiana died in 1955, she owned over a section (square mile) of land in Brazoria County, Texas, with valuable mineral rights, a quarter section in Lane County, Kansas, farmland in Iowa and seven parcels of land in Dade County, Florida (Miami Beach).

Ina (she went by Ina Diana in later life) drew up many wills. The will in effect at her death established the "Frank and Ina Brinton Educational and Charitable Trust".

The sale of Ina's household goods was held on September 26, 1957, with Victor Masson as Administrator of the estate. Mr. Masson's son, Daniel, approached local historian Michael Zahs to purchase Brinton items for $1,000. The collection contained many items that had not been at the estate sale and had been stored in Masson's basement for many years. It took three pickup loads to move the items. The collection included over 700 magic lantern slides, 150 films including

two by noted cinematographer George Melies, a roll top desk, and over 50 sound recordings.

The films were on the original nitrate-based film, which is highly flammable. They were considered so potentially dangerous that they could not be sent through the mail. The Library of Congress and American Film Institute had them sent by special courier to their laboratories. The films were transferred to safety film, and they retained a copy for their archives and returned a copy of the safety films to Zahs.

Beginning in 2013, Zahs donated the Brinton Collection to the Special Collections division of the University of Iowa. The collection included several films, over 700 magic lantern slides, numerous letters, documents and photographs.

Saving Brinton

Three filmmakers, John Richard, Andrew Sherburne and Tommy Haines of the Iowa City area made a documentary about the collection. The film, entitled *Saving Brinton,* had a private premier at the Ainsworth (Iowa) Opera House on June 1, 2017. The Brintons had shown magic lantern slides and films there over 100 years before. The official premier occurred on June 18. The official premier was held at the

American Film Institute meetings in silver Spring, Maryland on June 17, 2017, and in Washington D. C. on June 18.

Poster for the film *Saving Brinton*

Zahs and the filmmakers were invited to Begonia Italy for the oldest continuing film festival during the last week of June and first of July to show some of the Brinton films.

Saving Brinton has been entered in over 45 film festivals and has had over 120 screenings. It has been shown in Argentina, Belgium, Canada, China, England, Ethiopia, Greece, Italy, Sweden, Scotland, The Netherlands, Norway, and South Korea.

A one-hour version was featured on the national Public Television network.

The Brinton Trust

Frank Brinton died in December 1919, after an illness of over a year. His will, dated September of 1919, set up a trust to benefit Indiana and the Washington County Hospital.

> "The net income from the trust estate as it accrues shall be paid to my
>
> wife during life so long as she does not remarry. I desire that during this period my wife suitable (sic) and abundantly provided with care, maintenance, comfort and pleasures

satisfactory and appropriate to her station. And if her available income at any time becomes inadequate to furnish the same, then the additional funds required therefor may be taken from the principal of the trust estate and be used for such purpose. At the

death or remarriage of my wife the whole of the trust estate then remaining shall pass to the Washington County Hospital Association."

In her will of March 30, 1943, Ina set up the Frank and Indiana Brinton Trust. It was to be :

"A charitable, educational, and Christian organization eligible to receive benefits under this will shall specialize in the upbuilding of character and in assisting individuals to better understand life's purpose. My desire is to assist toward the attainment of Life 100% viz the purpose of Creation."

A previous will included the term "for the perpetuation of youth."

Ina did not have an attorney appointed for the trust, so it went to court and Judge Ira Morrison named his brother Gifford as attorney for the trust. Gifford was the trust's attorney for several years. Over the years, the trust has given many millions of dollars to support projects in Washington County, Iowa. It still generates about $99,000 each year. The Washington County Hospital always receives a part in the distribution of funds.

Frank and Indiana Brinton are likely the largest benefactors in the history of the

county. Education and heath are conditions used in distributing Brinton Trust monies.

Though often not understood, accepted, or appreciated by the community, and even their own family, Frank and Indiana Brinton continue to benefit the community.

BIBLIOGRAPHY

NEWSPAPERS

"At the Airdome", *Washington Evening Journal,* June 15, 1908, pg. 3, col. 3.

"At the Airdome", *Washington Evening Journal,* June 26, 1908, pg. 4, col. 1.

"Brinton Entertainment" *Washington Evening Journal,* November 12, 1897, pg.3, col.4.

"Card from Mr. J. Brinton", *The Press,* March 3, 1869, pg. 3. Col. 3.

"Jonathan Brinton", *The Press,* September 18, 1872, pg. Col. 2

"Letter from Texas", *Washington Evening Journal,* February 18, 1913, pg. 6, col. 1-3.

"Local Department", *The Press,* March 10, 1869, pg. 3. Col. 1.

"Mary Brinton", *The Brighton Enterprise,* May 3, 1902, Pg. 1, col. 2.

The Press, March 17, 1869, pg. 3. Col. 2.

"Stand From Under!", *The Press,* March 24, 1869, pg. 3. Col. 1.

Washington's First Aerial Navigation Agitator, *Washington Evening Journal,* September 27, 1919, full page.

Washington Democrat, November 11, 1902.

Washington Evening Journal, June 5, 1894, pg. 6, col. 2.

Washington Evening Journal, February 3, 1899.

Washington Evening Journal, April 2, 1907 pg. 2. Col. 3, 4.

Washington Evening Journal, March 28, 1912, pg. 8, col. 2 ,3.

Washington Evening Journal, June 8, 1904.

"Will be Up to Date", *Washington Evening*

Journal, Nov. 17, 1910, pg. 4, col. 3

"W.R.C.", *Washington Evening Journal*, June 8, 1894, pg.4. col. 3.

Sept 27,1919 pg. 5 duplicate of letter.

Journal March 3, 1933

CORRESPONDENCE

Brinton Jonathan letter to Frank Brinton, "and can you and me and everyone", no date.

Brinton Jonathan letter to Frank Brinton, "I have not received any notice" London 4th 1884.

Brinton Jonathan letter to George Brinton, "What I propose to do", no date.

Brinton Jonathan letter to George Brinton, "Now all you have to do", no date.

Brinton Jonathan letter, "When he chose unto himself", no date.

Brinton Jonathan letter, "I have a much brighter prospect", no date.

Brinton Jonathan letter to Nathan Brinton, "Nathan that $100 I want sent", no date.

Brinton Jonathan letter to Frank Brinton, "And do not disgrace yourselves", no date.

Brinton Jonathan letter to Mary Brinton, "All the stock and farming utensils", no date.

Brinton Jonathan letter to one of his sons, "deeds recorded before my death", no date.

Brinton Jonathan letter to Frank Brinton, "I receive thy letter", London, April 8, 1884

Brinton Jonathan to unknown recipient, "More for him than he had sense for", no date.

Ranney, Mark to Mary Brinton, "It is true your husband is uneasy and restless." March 14, 1870.

PUBLISHED LEAFLETS

"Notice is hereby Given" by Jonathan Brinton, London, no date.
"Wanted by his Relatives", no date.

BOOKS

Ingham, Brinton genealogy

MISC

Court document #630, Clerk of Court Office, Washington County Iowa Courthouse.

Funeral receipt C. S. Woodford Undertaking Parlors

Probate Record, Book E, pg. 190
Probate Record, Book K, pg. 615